THIS PUBLICATION HAS BEEN CREATED
BY DACORUM HERITAGE
AS PART OF THE
A TASTE OF OVALTINE PROJECT
FUNDED BY
THE GARFIELD WESTON FOUNDATION
AND ARTS COUNCIL ENGLAND

CONTENTS

5 FOREWORD
by Peter Roth, former staff member and current curator of the local archives at Wander AG, Switzerland

6 INTRODUCTION
to the Ovaltine Collection at Dacorum Heritage

8 LANDSCAPES
   11 FARMS
   14 THE SWISS INFLUENCE

16 HEALTH AND WELLBEING
   23 BALLS UNDER THE BALLROOM
   26 OVALTIMES

27 PROCESSES
   37 HEALTH AND SAFETY
   38 THE WORLD'S MOST POPULAR FOOD BEVERAGE

39 PRODUCTS
   45 ROYAL SEALS OF APPROVAL

46 ADVERTISING
   49 THE OVALTINE MAID
   54 SPORTS AND SPONSORSHIP
   56 THE OVALTINEYS

57 CLOSURE
   58 RESCUE OF THE ARCHIVE

59 ACKNOWLEDGEMENTS

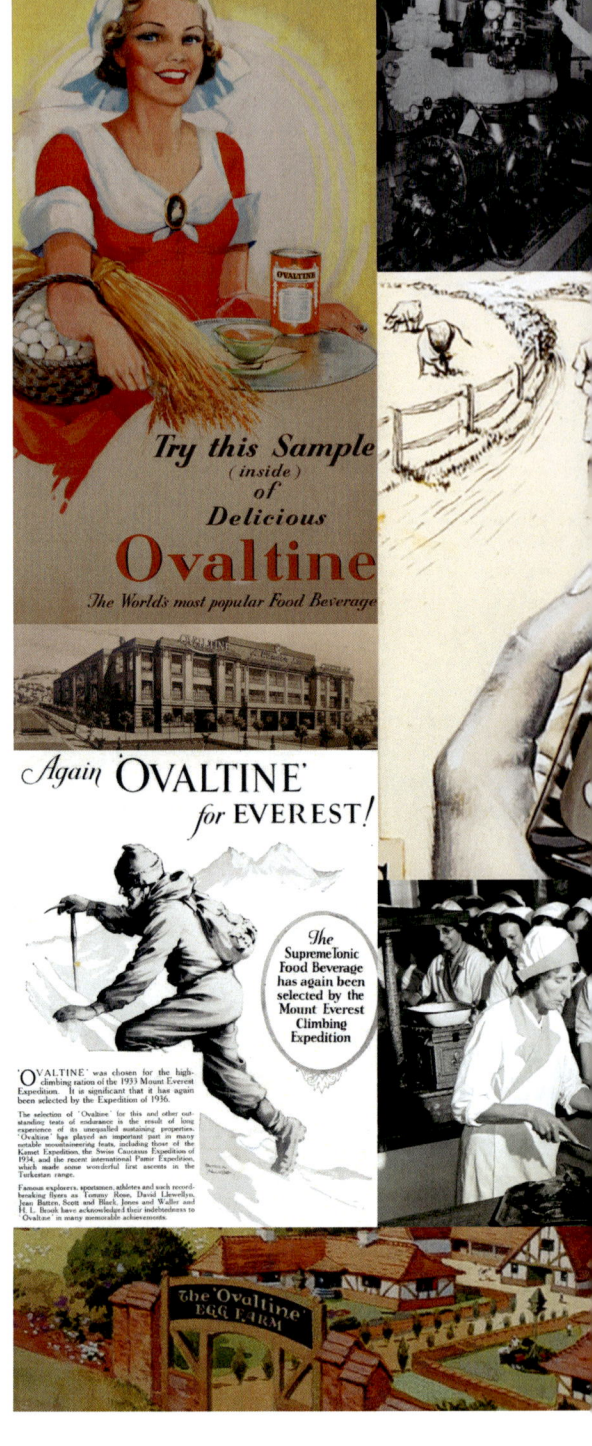

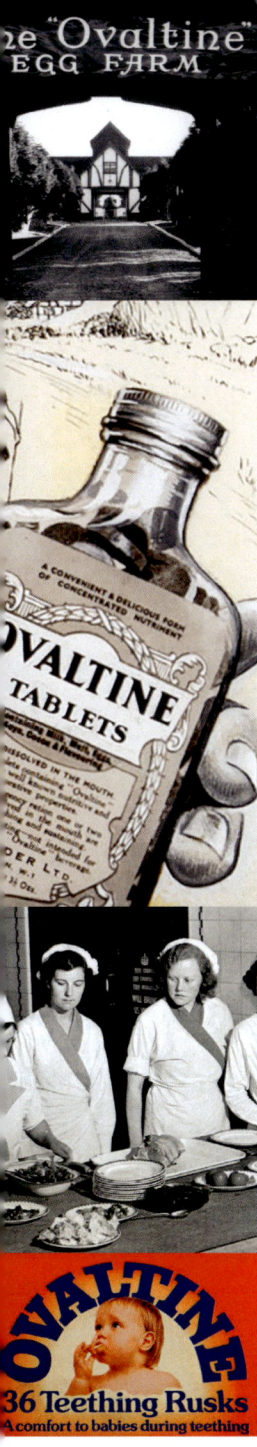

FOREWORD

This book you're holding is a living monument to a company rich in tradition that has touched the lives of many people. The story of Ovaltine in Kings Langley is one of commitment, community and pride in one's work. When the factory closed in 2002, former employees preserved many objects, documents and personal memories –silent witnesses to almost 100 years of company history.

The Dacorum Heritage Trust has taken great care to record, archive and bring to life this valuable material. Particularly noteworthy is the recent addition of eyewitness interviews, which provide a deeply moving insight into everyday working life, company culture and the feelings of the people who were the heart and soul of this history. This little book is the result of this dedicated work.

It is a 'printed museum' that focuses not only on objects, but above all on the voices and experiences of people. It is a story of pride, cohesion and changing times – preserving an important chapter in the region's industrial history.

The fact that the Ovaltine brand is still part of many people's everyday lives gives this collection a special relevance. It shows how strong the roots of a brand can be – supported by the work, knowledge and passion of generations.

The memories captured here are a treasure for the present and a bridge to the past – a legacy that touches, inspires and keeps alive the cultural identity of a region.

Peter Roth, Former staff member and current curator of the
local archives at the historical headquarters of Wander AG,
Neuenegg, Switzerland

▷ Oil painting of an Ovaltine Rusk advert from the factory board room. Artist: Leon Sprinck.

THE OVALTINE ARCHIVE

Dacorum Heritage cares for over 10,000 objects from the Ovaltine Factory in Kings Langley. The collection spans the twentieth century, beginning from the factory's early days in the 1910s to its closure in 2002. It is made up of a diverse range of materials – from exquisite oil paintings that once hung in the factory meeting rooms to radio and TV advertising, uniforms, office documents, and products. Dacorum Heritage has recently added to this archive by gathering oral histories from ex-employees. From these, we gain an insight into the working lives of the people within Ovaltine's production lines, offices and laboratories.

In this short book, we are delighted to share the collection in the form of a 'printed exhibition', highlighting objects and the stories they tell.

The oral history quotes included in this publication are taken from the transcripts of interviews. These have been edited to appear in written language while retaining the spirit of speech.

"Reels and reels of film, lots of lovely paintings, original paintings they used for advertising in those days."
Linda Lythaby, Print Room, 1960s–1990s.

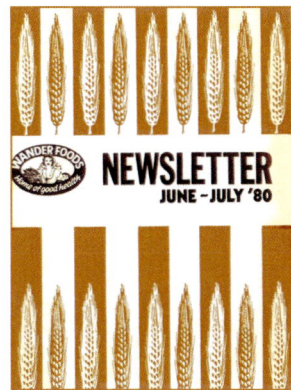

Δ A staff newsletter from 1980.

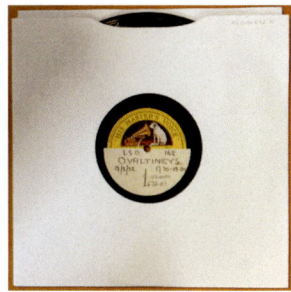

Δ An LP of the Ovaltineys Radio Show from 1938.

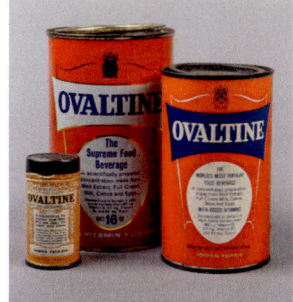

Δ Ovaltine tins from the collection.

No. 106647

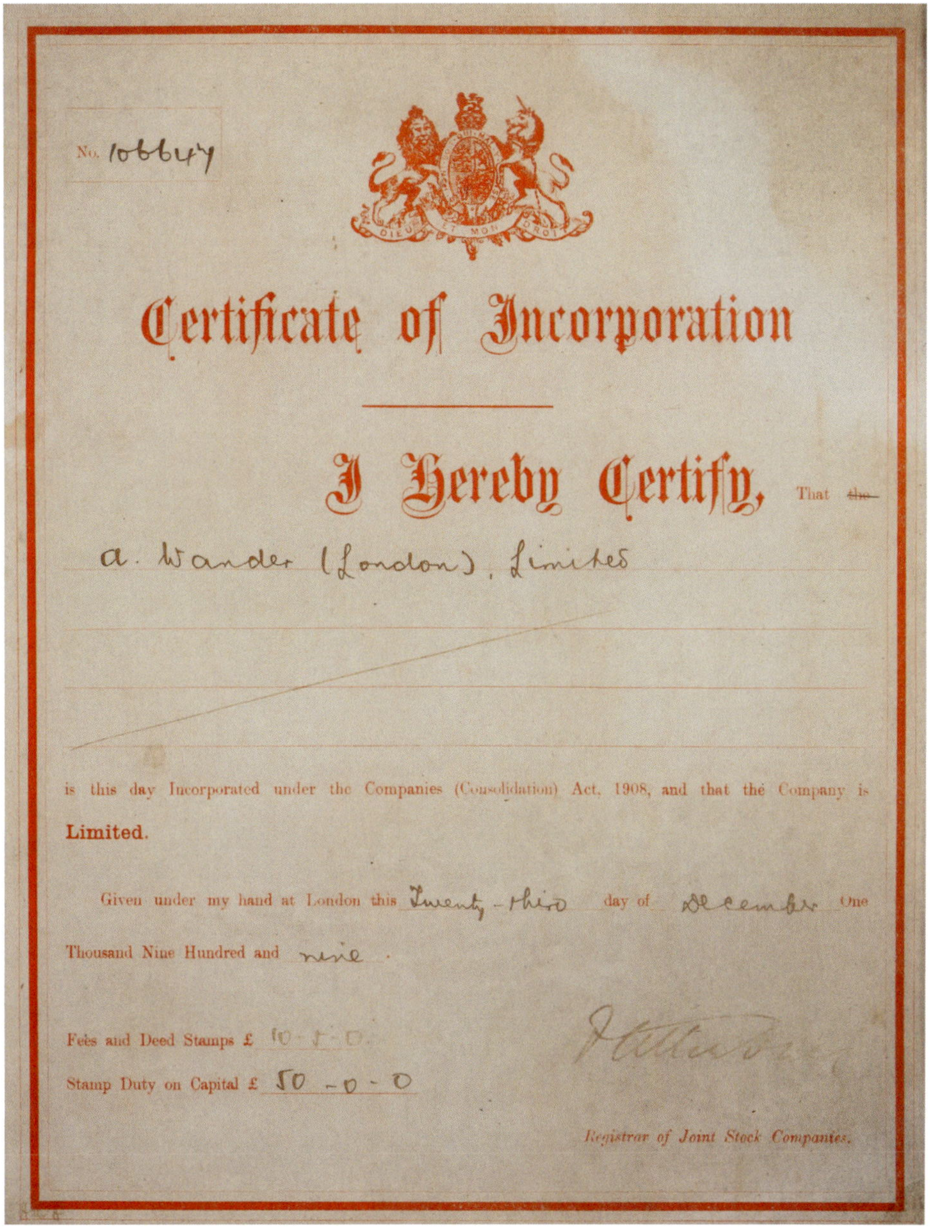

Certificate of Incorporation

I Hereby Certify, That ~~the~~

A. Wander (London), Limited

is this day Incorporated under the Companies (Consolidation) Act, 1908, and that the Company is

Limited.

Given under my hand at London this Twenty-third day of December One Thousand Nine Hundred and nine.

Fees and Deed Stamps £ 10-5-0.

Stamp Duty on Capital £ 50-0-0

Registrar of Joint Stock Companies.

Δ Certificate of Incorporation of A. Wander (London) Limited, creator and owner of Ovaltine, dated 23 December 1909.

△ 'What an ideal spot for a food factory!' states a company booklet. In the late 1920s, the factory building was extravagantly expanded into an Art Deco landmark, in the heart of Kings Langley.

LANDSCAPES

▽ Our first image of the original two-storey Ovaltine factory comes from 1913. Inside worked a staff of about 13.

"Big and impressive...the frontage on it...Art Deco...was lovely. Above the door, I remember there being a blue and red oval shaped thing which had 'A.W.' on it. It was moulded. It wasn't stuck on."

Roy Platten of the Print Studio on his first impressions of the factory in the 1970s.

8 - LANDSCAPES

The building may have acquired a stylish front, but it was always described as a 'factory in a country garden'. In documents and images from the 1920s onwards, the factory is commonly drawn or painted, surrounded by the fields and farms that produced the key ingredients for Ovaltine – milk, eggs and barley.

A booklet from the factory's early decades, entitled 'The Home of Good Health', describes 'a countryside of soft wooded hills, quaint, old-fashioned villages and lovely parks' as the 'chosen site' for the 'ideal food factory'.

A black and white Ovaltine company film explains that,
'The coal to power the extensive plant of the factory is brought by canal from the midlands on the firm's own narrow boats. There are many barges in constant use, but despite this grimy cargo, the canal folk keep the boats on which they and their families live spick and span, worthy of being the fleet to power the home of good health.'

Coal was delivered on Ovaltine narrow boats on the Grand Union Canal which flowed directly next to the factory.

Railway passengers to London would have been able to take in this pastoral production line, and the railway was vital for the supply of tin and other products used in manufacturing.

Good transport links, a plentiful supply of water, and a workforce from nearby towns and villages are some of the reasons proposed for why Ovaltine came to this corner of Dacorum, Kings Langley.

△ The Ovaltine Egg Farm on Egg Farm Lane, a short walk from the factory.

△ From a 1960s company film, also named 'The Home of Good Health', showing a bus full of visitors arriving at the Ovaltine Farms.

FARMS

In 1929, the company purchased two local farms to create an Ovaltine Egg and Dairy Farm to supply fresh ingredients to the factory. In the spring and summer, members of the public, such as school groups and the Women's Institute, were able to visit the farms located in Kings and Abbots Langley, as well as the factory itself. Visitors were given tours around the thatched and timbered farm buildings, some of which were said to be based on Marie Antoinette's model hamlet at the Palace of Versailles. Visitors were encouraged to admire the 'aristocratic' pedigree of the prize-winning Jersey Cows and White Leghorn hens chosen to produce the 'highest quality' Ovaltine ingredients.

△ The Ovaltine Dairy Farm on Dairy Way, Abbots Langley.

△ A thatcher working on one of the Ovaltine Egg Farm buildings, with a view of the factory and railway line in the background, circa 1969. Photo by Ray Daniells.

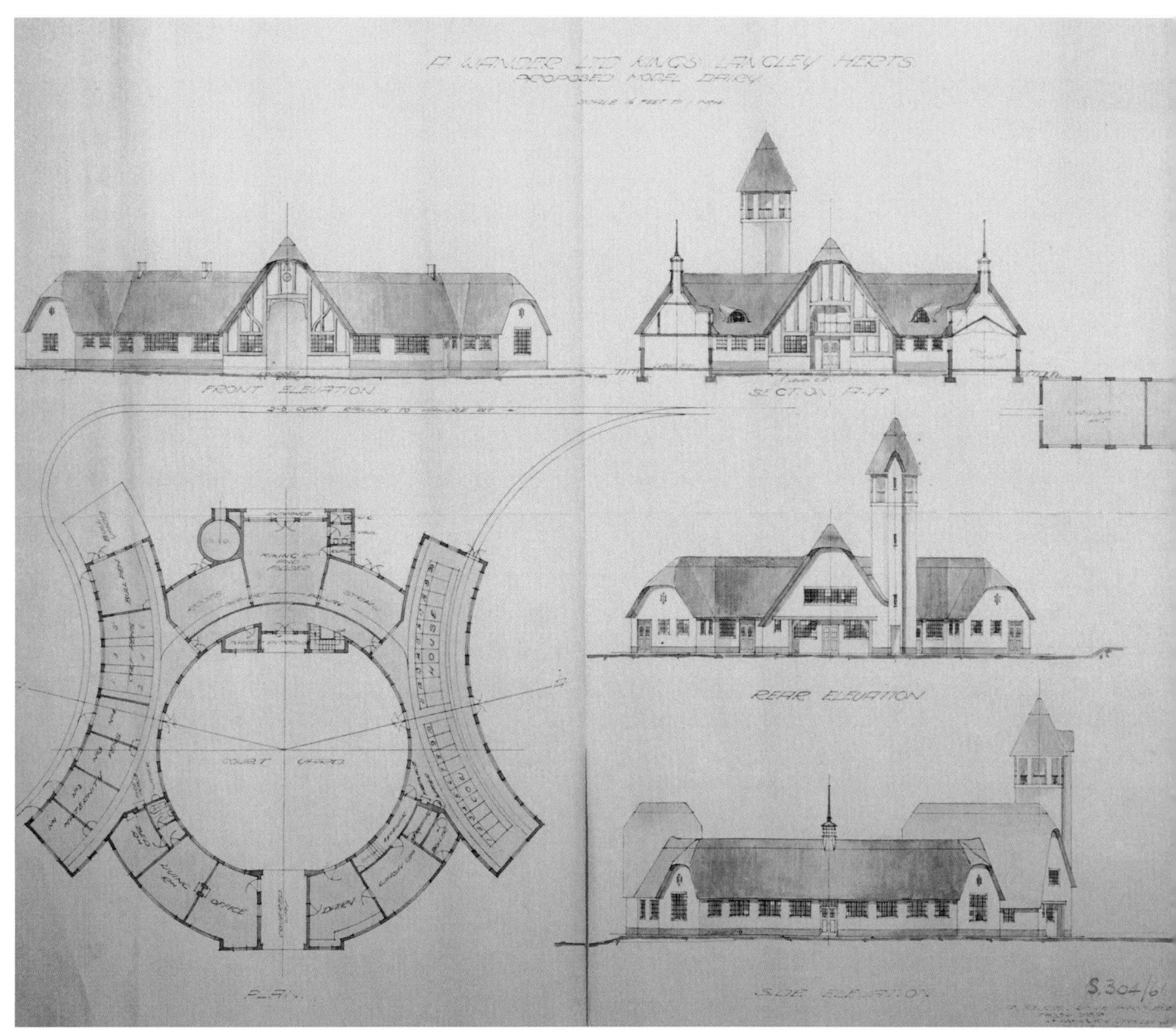

△ Hand-drawn architectural plans for the Proposed Model Dairy Farm by Bowden Son & Partners Architects from 1932. It includes details of the Cow House such as the maternity pens, straw storage and living accommodation for the farmer.

THE SWISS INFLUENCE

Ovaltine has its origins in Switzerland with the Wander family in the 19th century. Although we may think of Ovaltine and Kings Langley as inextricably linked, throughout its existence the factory had Swiss owners.

In 1865, Dr George Wander, a Swiss chemist, set up a laboratory in Berne to combat the widespread problem of malnutrition. He struck upon a natural product: barley malt. Impressed with its nutritional qualities, especially as a food for children, Dr Wander commenced manufacture of a long-lasting malt extract. While nutritious, the original extract was not delicious. Dr Wander's son, Albert Wander, continued to develop the core ingredient, combining it with milk, eggs and cocoa to refine the taste. Ovomaltine was placed on the market in Switzerland in 1904. The product was exported to the UK in 1906, where it was called Ovaltine.

The Ovaltine Factory in Kings Langley was owned by a succession of Swiss companies: by Ovaltine's founders known as Wander Limited, then Sandoz Limited in 1967, and Novartis from 1996.

◁ Father and son creators of Ovaltine, George Wander and Albert Wander. The surname Wander appears in many documents and objects associated with the Kings Langley Factory.

The Kings Langley factory may have been geographically set apart from its Swiss owners, however, the influence of the 'Swiss style' of business was felt by the workers in Kings Langley and through its management.

"The Swiss way was if anything becomes a significant dispute it was regarded as a management failure. The management would be held responsible. The Swiss way, still today, is you're managing the site, you're responsible for everything. If something gets out of hand then the management, the upper management in Switzerland, would want to know how did this happen? There are obviously indicators that this was going to go wrong and the management should have stepped in and changed it... It might not be done speedily, but it would be done correctly. And if you live in Switzerland, which I have done, that is the ethos there, it will be done right. It's a matter of personal reputation in Switzerland."
Peter Addison, Quality Management, 1970s-2000s.

For most of the factory's existence, from 1909 until the 1970s, there had been a Head or City Office in London. The premises of the offices changed, depending on the size of the operation. Its most lavish base was 184 Queens Gate, Kensington. Photographs of the interiors, with their palm trees and oil paintings, have the air of a private club. The building was demolished by a bomb in the Second World War.

◁ The exterior of the City Office at 184 Queens Gate, Kensington, taken in January 1932.

LANDSCAPES - 15

△ This colourised black and white photo taken in the 1920s shows the outdoor gardens and leisure spaces for the Ovaltine workers.

HEALTH AND WELLBEING

Ovaltine promises nutrition and vitality to its consumers. From a 1920s newspaper advert that claims that 'one cup of Ovaltine contains more nourishment than 12 cups of beef extract, 7 cups of cocoa or 3 eggs', to the Ovaltiney radio broadcast in March 1937, urging mothers to keep giving Ovaltine to their children 'to build up resistance to colds and infections', a focus on health is at the heart of the product.

This concern for health and wellbeing also extended to those making Ovaltine – the factory workers in Kings Langley.

Stand outside the factory in the early-to-mid-twentieth century and you would see gardens, tennis courts and bowling greens for the employees.

△ Workers relaxing by the tennis courts circa 1930.

◁ A Ladies Tennis Tournament Trophy 1952–1955.

'The health and happiness of the workers is a matter of keen interest to the manufacturers of Ovaltine…The workers feel they are part of a great enterprise. They give of their best in return for all that is done to make work pleasant and happy for them.'
Home of Good Health Booklet.

Ovaltine workers were invited to join sports teams, representing the company and winning trophies. Inter-departmental matches could be fraught events when office and factory staff came head-to-head.

△ The Ovaltine Netball Team, 1967. Photo by Roger King.

"We used to have the inter-departmental six-a-side football matches and there was always friction. The guys in the tin shop wanted to get the suits…I took out one guy in a match, and he jumped up, not realising it was me, looking for a fight. I said sorry and he said, 'Oh, it's you Roy, that's OK.' If it had been anyone else, that would have been fists."
Roy Platten, Print Studio, 1970s & 1990s.

△ The Ovaltine Football Team, 1969.

HEALTH AND WELLBEING · 17

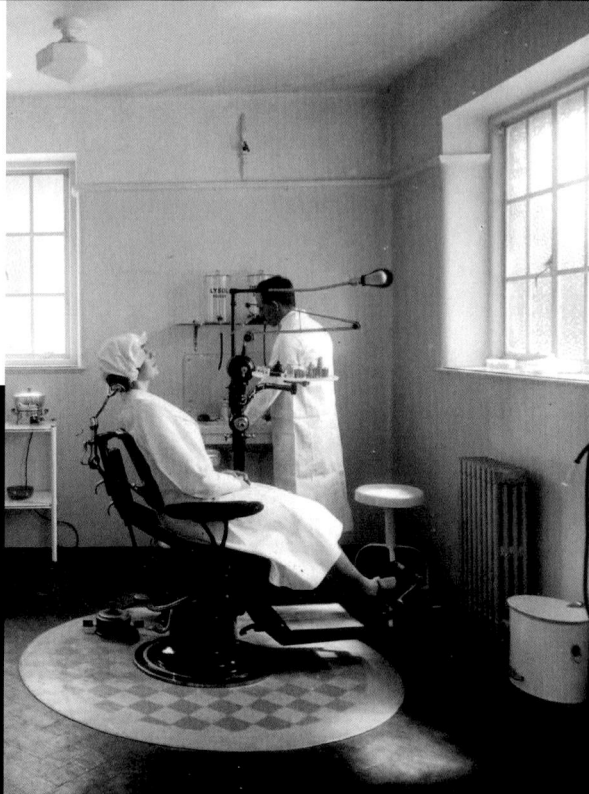

Enter the factory and you find other 'welfare facilities.' These included a 'Sun Ray Room' in the early decades, where staff could enjoy the 'vitalising influence' of ultra-violet rays. Medical professionals were on site to care for the employees and to provide routine check-ups – a service that was offered for much of the factory's existence.

"They had a good medical side too because the dentist used to come to the factory and a chiropodist, and a lady used to come to check the women... The blood bank used to come to the factory so you could give blood. So, nobody lost time going for these appointments."
Linda Lythaby, Print Room, 1960s–1990s.

18 - HEALTH AND WELLBEING

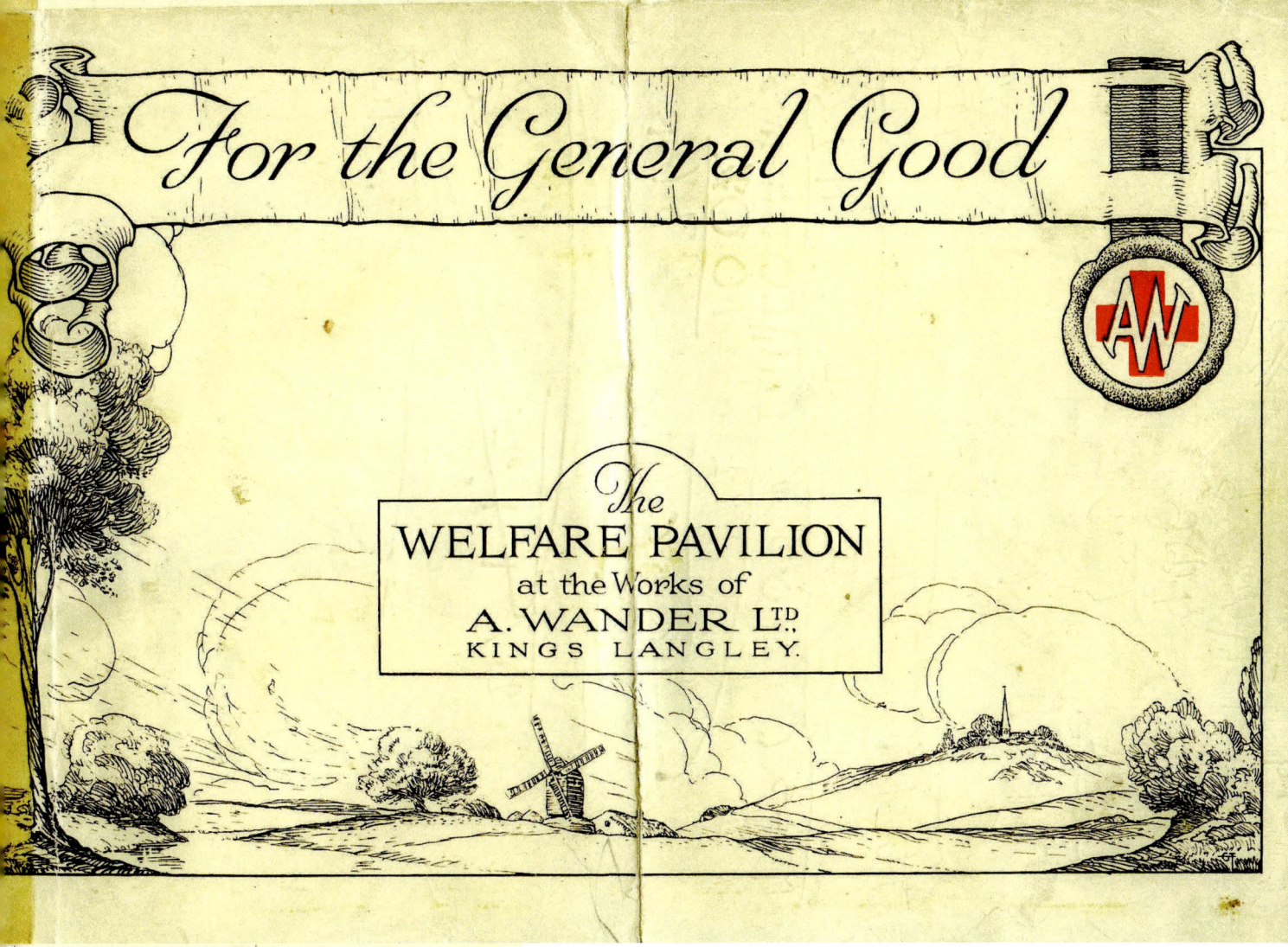

To Avoid Epidemics

In this way epidemics are started, and we realise that an epidemic at a factory such as ours may become a great danger; it may not only involve the lives of many employees, but may be the means of spreading the disease amongst many of the employees' families and their friends.

We therefore consider it essential in the interests of our employees and the general public to take every precaution that is humanly possible against such epidemics, and—if they do occur—to see they do not spread. So when we urge our staff to consult the Welfare Pavilion doctor immediately they feel "out-of-sorts," we are not making a mountain out of a molehill. A sore throat may be only a sore throat. A bilious attack may be only a bilious attack. If they are simple ailments a simple treatment will do no harm. But if, on the other hand, they are—to the experienced eye of a doctor—the beginnings of an infectious illness or disease, then many workers in all departments may be saved serious—even dangerous—illness.

In Case of Accidents

The Welfare Pavilion has been built and equipped to meet all kinds of emergencies, not the least of them being the treatment of wounds. For it is realised that even trivial wounds or burns need proper medical attention for the avoidance of blood poisoning—one of the very easiest complaints to contract even in the cleanliest surroundings—and that the expert dressing and cleansing of a wound can save weeks of dangerous illness and absence from work. The surgery is also equipped for the treatment of severe injuries.

A booklet for the on-site 'Welfare Pavilion' from the early twentieth century shows where the medical and health facilities were located. It is described as a 'miniature hospital'. The booklet reveals that the company was highly aware of the danger of 'epidemics' spreading through such an extensive workforce, which would come to reach almost 1,500 employees in the 1950s.

△ Photo taken by Mr Sanger of Life Magazine in 1940.

"When I first started in the early-to-mid 70s, people used to go to the pub every lunch time, you know. It was the culture like that...You'd think nothing of going there for two or three pints and something to eat. That probably died out in the early part of the 80s and quite rightly really in hindsight, but that was part of the social side which sometimes went on until the evenings."
Nick Brodrick, Purchasing, 1970s–2000s.

◁ The Red Lion, one of the pubs near the Ovaltine factory and a place for lunch and a drink.

There were allotted breaks for staff, with a tea break in the morning, and a canteen that served meals to the workers.

"They had three canteens. They had one for the workers, which were the factory workers, one for staff. And then they had a waitress service for managers. I mean, you wouldn't get that nowadays, would you? And it was all subsidised as well."
Roger King, Accounts Department, recalling the canteen in the 1960s.

Ovaltine had an organised and lively social club that was open to all departments. Activities ranged from day trips to the seaside to visits to the theatre and sports outings.

"I also used to belong to the fishing club…so we used to get free trips out a couple of times a year. We had fishing matches in the company."
Ken Allum, Manufacturing, 1980s–2000s.

"We had some day trips when I first started there. The one I remember we went across to France for the day. Quite a long, old day. All four of us in the print room went on that one. It was hours across the Channel. Didn't have long in Boulogne, really."
Linda Lythaby, Print Room, recalling an overseas trip from the 1960s.

"Part of Personnel and HR was the staff shop, of course, which sold Ovaltine products at vastly reduced prices. They used to sell promotional items as well."
Peter Addison, Quality Management, 1970s–2000s.

◁ Janette Noonan from the Ovaltine Shop, receiving a certificate for a charity initiative.

Janette Noonan took over the running of the shop from her mother in the 1980s.

Were all departments equal in all ways? Sometimes the perks did not feel evenly spread.

▽ L: Doris Davies, a casual helper, R: Violet Dicker (Janette's mother), in the Ovaltine Shop.

"There was a lot of friction between sales and marketing and the people that worked in the factory. It was the small things that rankled with people. The toilets in the factory had the old-fashioned Izal toilet paper and apparently it was because the drains and sewage couldn't cope. But in the terrapin building [the offices] they had soft stuff and it was those small divides that made a big difference to people."
Roy Platten, Print Studio, 1970s & 1990s.

HEALTH AND WELLBEING - 21

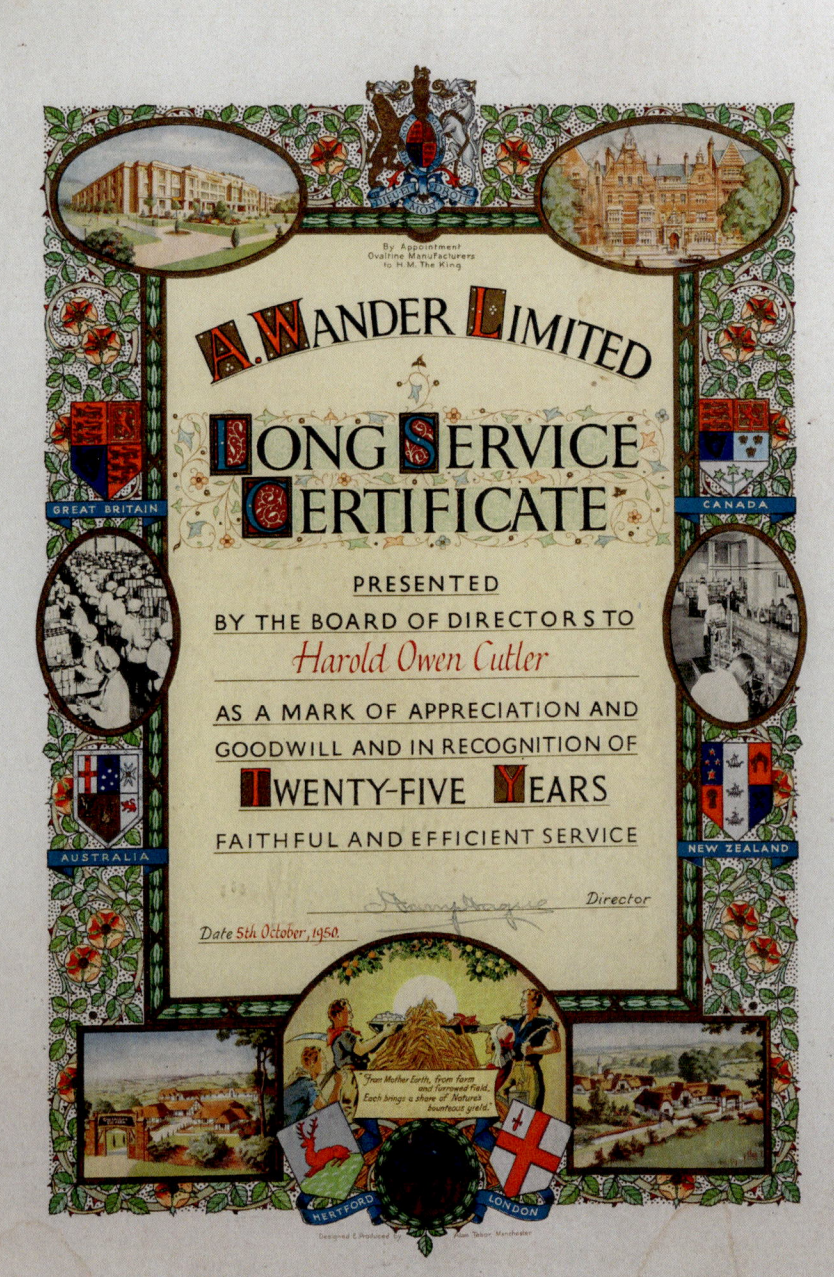

Anniversaries of years of service were published in the company's employee newsletter. A further boost to morale was the creation of a 25 Years Club. Members received a beautifully illustrated certificate from the Board of Directors.

For those who retired from Ovaltine, there was the pensioners club, with its dinners, meet-ups and holidays.

◁ A long service certificate from 1950.

"They always used to have pensioners' dinners, and you had to be in those days, [as] a pensioner. I think they had pensioners' holidays as well. They used to go away for a week's holiday, the lot of them."
Linda Lythaby, Print Room, 1960s–1990s.

PARTY TIME

BALLS UNDER THE BALLROOM

One other facility to be enjoyed by staff for much of Ovaltine's existence was the ballroom. This space was used for social and cultural events – from rock 'n' roll bands to fashion shows to horticultural competitions and children's parties. Staff Christmas parties were also held in the ballroom in the early days and these could be particularly colourful, as shown in this double page photo of the party of December 1963.

△ Photo from the staff Ovaltimes newsletter from January 1964.

HEALTH AND WELLBEING - 23

△ Close up of exquisite, coloured glass from the Ovaltine ballroom windows. Photo by Roy Platten.

'People lined the bar six deep. The noise was tremendous as there was so much to talk about, one would have thought we were all lost relatives meeting for the first time, 'what a nice dress', 'look at so-and-so talking to so-and-so', 'who'd have thought he'd come with her?' Upstairs the dance floor was packed. The youngsters twisted and shook, while those who preferred a more sedate form of dancing were able to foxtrot and waltz.'
Ovaltimes account of the Christmas party of 1964, written by Madeline Hutchings.

"It was really lovely, dancing, free food, free drink. They cared for us and made you feel valuable. They gave everyone a turkey and we got a Christmas bonus as well. It was like a big family getting together and having fun. That actually made you want to do good work for them because you felt very valued."
Beverley Platten, Costings, 1970s–1980s.

"Every lunchtime in the winter time they'd open up the ballroom and they had a record-player so all the youngsters used to go up there. Boys used to sit on one side, the girls on the other. They'd play the records and all the girls would dance to The Beatles and things like that."
Roger King, Accounts, 1960s.

"We never knew why it was a sprung floor until the day they demolished the ballroom. We found out that what they'd put under the wood floor was tennis balls. They used a ball and chain to demolish it and as soon as it hit the floor all these tennis balls flew out. The builders didn't know what to do. Then we realised how they sprung the floor and none of us knew before then."
Peter Addison, Quality Management, 1970s–2000s.

The ballroom was particularly suited to dancing, but for many years what lay beneath its well-sprung floor was a mystery.

Even professional dancers were drawn to the space, with many ballroom dancing competitions held at the factory in the 1950s and 1960s.

OVALTIMES

Ovaltine produced a regular newsletter for its workers in Kings Langley. The contents ranged from company achievements and announcements to details specific to the Kings Langley workers: weddings, births, lists of 'anniversaries' showing years of service, and social news. In-jokes and cartoons kept the tone warm-hearted.

In style and content, the newsletters offer an insight into the changing work culture over the decades and under the different owners of the factory. The early front covers often included illustrations by print studio staff. By the 2000s, the Ovaltine factory is part of the pharmaceuticals conglomerate Novartis and the people of the Kings Langley factory are no longer the sole focus of the company newsletter.

"The Ovaltine newsletters... had to be out I think on the third week of the month and normally we didn't get anything until the second week of the month. Most of the publications were 24–32 pages. So to get that art work plated, printed, folded, stapled and trimmed was a mammoth task on that third week of every month. On the newsletter, there had been Duncan, myself, Edna and Brenda, so four probably, and we had our hands to the pump. The newsletters were all folded by hand, every sheet that came off had to be folded by hand, collated by hand, stapled by hand. There was no machinery to do all that."

Roy Platten recalls preparing the newsletter in the Ovaltine print studio from 1974–78 when there were roughly 750 workers at the factory.

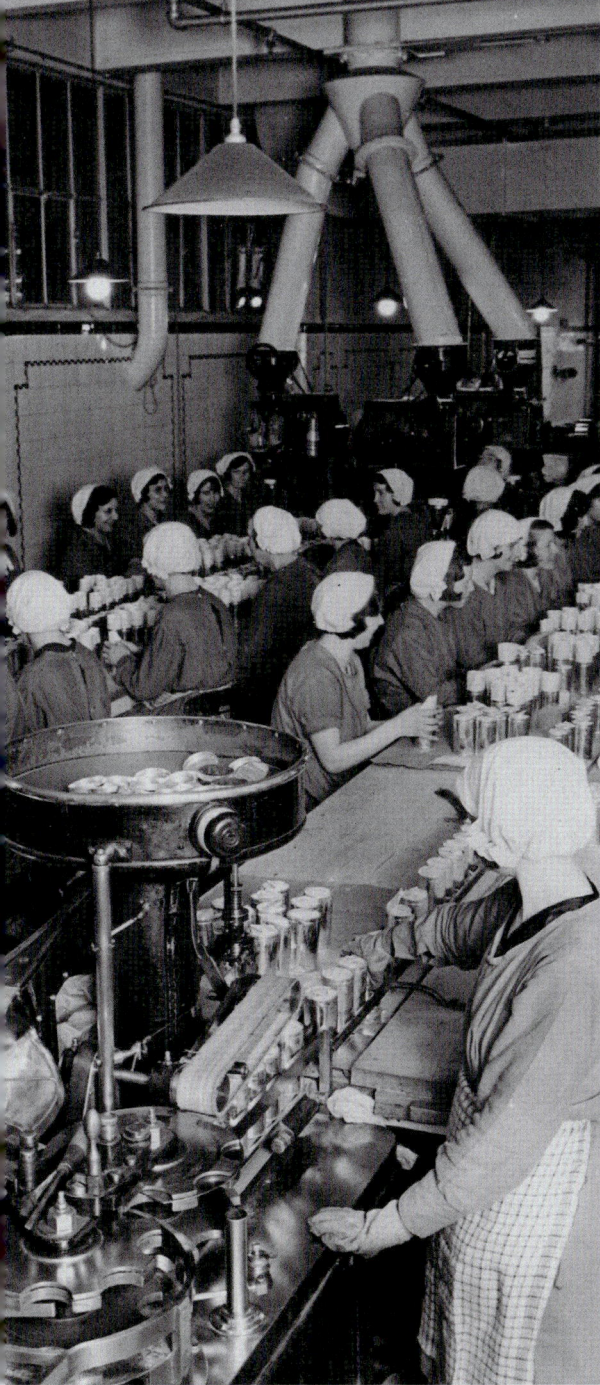
△ The Ovaltine Packing Room circa 1932.

PROCESSES

On the outside – and for brand purposes – Ovaltine may seem like a drink made in a bucolic and sociable idyll. However, there was still hard work to be done, with carefully calibrated and scientific procedures to follow to maintain the quality of the product.

"I mean the first thing I recall when I started was when I was walking into the entrance after you'd gone past the security gate house, as you go towards the factory – and it's probably still like that now – there were two entrances. One had a stone carving over the top saying Office Entrance and the other said Works Entrance, as though you were supposed to go a certain way to access different parts of the building. It wasn't that simple when you got inside. It was a bit more of a labyrinth inside. That's the first thing that stuck in my mind."
Nick Brodrick, Purchasing, 1970s–2000s.

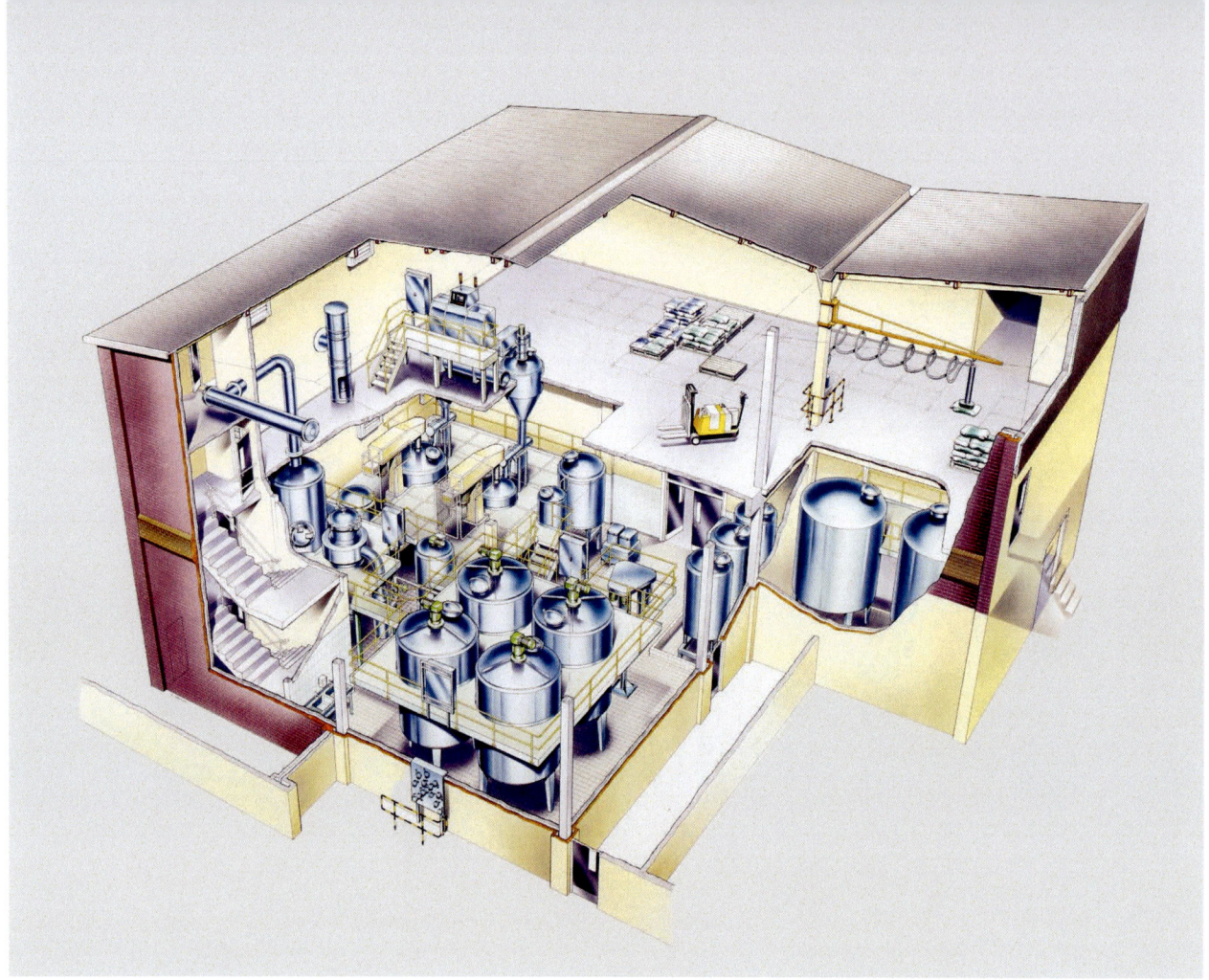

△ Interior view of Ovaltine manufacturing machinery.

The manufacturing of Ovaltine was a 24/7 procedure.

Ken Allum, a Shift Supervisor from the 1980s–2000s, remembers that there were about "eight men per shift, to cover each phase of production."

"Sometimes you ended up doing a double shift because the guy who was due to come in, if he goes sick, then you'd be asked to cover another shift. It was a continuous process."

The shift workers operated enormous machinery to turn the product from a syrup state to a dried biscuit-like form. There were "eight band driers and they must have been 10ft high and they ran for 30 to 40ft long."

Then, as Ken remembers, there was "the panel four, which basically went from the ground floor to the top of the building where it was brought out from a vacuum to atmospheric pressures, and it went back down to the tote room, where it went through the granulators to make the actual Ovaltine itself in the tote bins and those tote bins would go up to the packing room, where they filled the different tins with Ovaltine."

"If you were unlucky, and you got a breakdown on the ovens, that got hot, and that was pretty unpleasant. When you got into the packing room and tin shop, you got conveyor belts and fast-moving equipment and tins and food going all sorts of ways."
Ted Luck, Mechanical Engineer, 1980s–1990s.

For the engineers in charge of maintaining the machines, it was a fast, skilled job.

△ The Tin Shop, where Ovaltine made its own tins, back in 1932.

MEMORIES OF THE TIN SHOP

"I liked the Tin Shop…I had my own slitter, which had massive bits of tin plate that came in on the pallets and you'd put them through the slitter and then the slitter would cut it into the measurement of the tin."
Dee Mayling, Factory Worker, 1980s.

The Tin Shop "made a huge amount of noise like something out of Dickens. It was incredibly loud and a bit like the cotton mill footage that you sometimes see of women, they were mostly women, mouthing stuff to each other because they couldn't hear over the noise of the machines."
Nick Brodrick, Purchasing, 1970s–2000s.

"The Tin Shop was very noisy, especially in the summer. Protected shoes, ear defenders, hats, overalls to be worn at all times. We had several machine fitters as machines often broke down."
Jan Porter, Tin Shop, evening shift and seasonal work, 1970s–1980s.

PROCESSES - 29

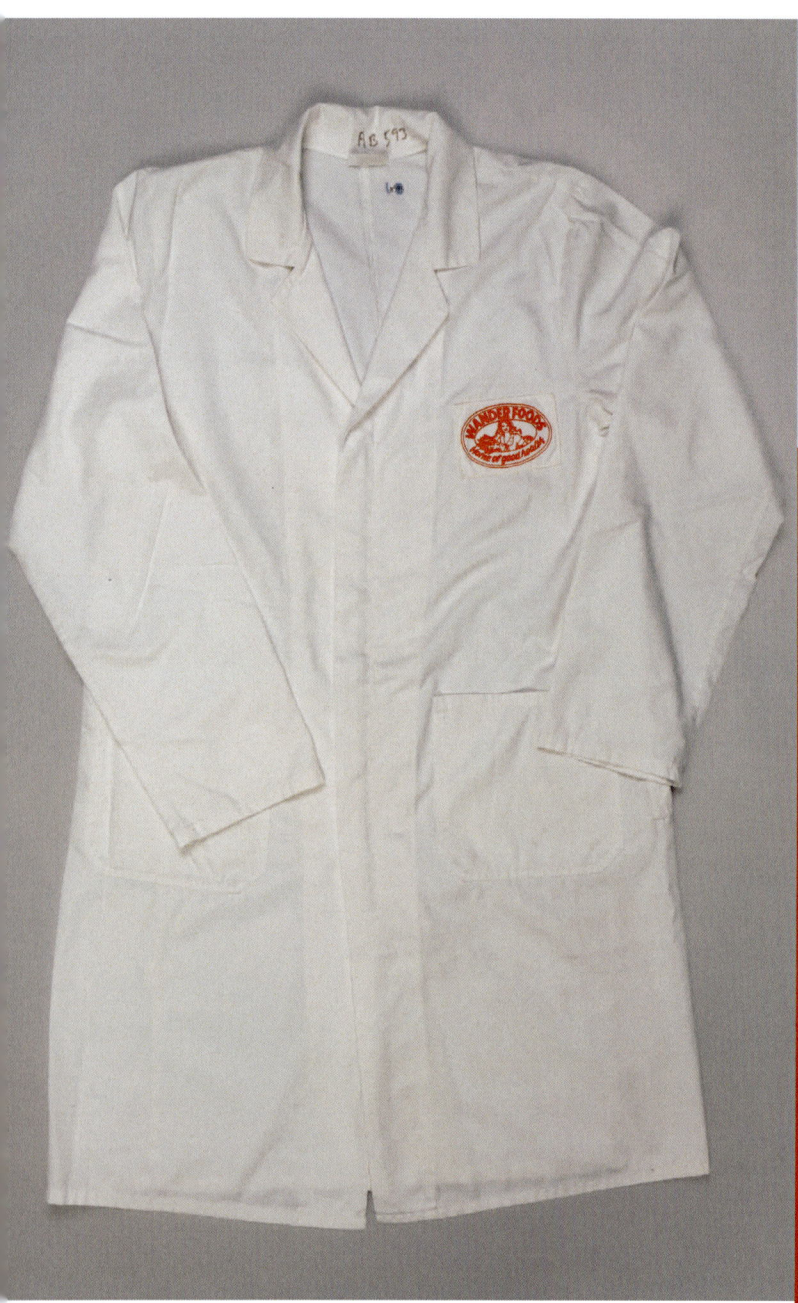

After manufacturing, Ovaltine had to pass through quality assurance checks.

◁ A white overall which would be worn by staff working in the factory and quality assurance laboratories.

The auto-analyser, "could do immense work. It could do a full analysis of moisture, protein, fat and ash for the product that would take one person one day to do. This thing could do that analysis 60 times a second. So it sounds great. It's automation and I was delighted. It cost about £90,000 and we thought it would revolutionise it. Well, it did. It actually found every mistake we produced. And so we had a lot of rejections of product. Then we had to deal with why we had all these rejections, and the Ovaltine was in my experience a very special place in that everyone pulled together. We found the problem and then we helped the guys working in manufacturing to find the answer and resolve it. Within two years, we had a very smooth product coming out at the end, with hardly any rejections. We had to go through that initial pain, though. But it was very satisfying for us and for the men in the factory. No one likes failure."

Peter Addison, Quality Management, 1970s–2000s.

Noise, scents, cigarette smoke and heat meant that being in the factory could be an intense experience for the senses.

▷ Checking the air-conditioning plant in 1932.

"I started in the bakery, and I thought it was cakes, but it was beer, the old Geordie beer. You had these hops on one side of you and I didn't wear gloves or anything like that. You'd go into the hops, you'd lift all these hops out, and you'd put it in the homebrew kits. And at the end of the day all you could smell was hops, all down your fingers."
Dee Mayling, when Ovaltine expanded to making Home Brew Kits, 1980s, (see page 44).

PROCESSES · 31

MEMORIES OF THE FACTORY OFFICES

The purchasing office in the 1970s "wasn't massive, and I didn't smoke, but five of the other six did, including one guy who was my immediate boss in the first phase, who smoked a pipe that was incredibly pungent. And there would be cigarettes tossed between the ladies of the office who were there as typists and secretaries and so forth. So, it was quite a fug and three months later I started as well, so..."
Nick Brodrick, Purchasing, 1970s–2000s.

"The girl operated a machine that printed the details onto cheques, which from memory was a large monster of a machine, almost the size of a whole desk. Why we were sending out cheques and to whom I have no memory at all. This girl was going to take a day release course, and I was chosen to fill in for her on the day she was off studying. I hate hot rooms and so this was an absolute ordeal for me, made worse by the rather unpleasant atmosphere created by the personnel in that room who barely spoke to me or to each other."
Sue Chandler, Customer Orders, 1960s.

"We had sugar bowls dotted around the office for when the tea lady came round. I tell you what, you'd look forward to her because people worked non-stop. There was no banter or anything. You'd just come in at half past eight and you worked till tea break time. And if you were talking, Old Wainwright would knock on the window. She'd [the tea lady] would come round and you'd have a cheese roll and a coffee and she used to shout Rosie Lee as she walked in."
Roger King, Accounts, 1960s.

△ Accounts Trainee Roger King tries out the boss's chair, 1964.

△ A balance from the Ovaltine Quality Assurance Laboratory before the introduction of digital equipment.

MEMORIES OF FACTORY EQUIPMENT

In its first decades, Ovaltine may have been able to boast of its state-of-the-art facilities. However, for those joining the workforce after the second half of the century, the once modern factory could have a distinctly antiquated look.

"My very first time around the factory, I was quite surprised how old it was. It wasn't a modern, high-tech place. Obviously, the machinery was, but the building itself was quite old."
Jacqueline Parsons, Wages Department, on her first impressions in 1979.

"In the early days the studio was really old world. He used to paint, the chap then. He used to do a lot of hand painting and silk screening."
Linda Lythaby, Print Studio, 1960s–1990s.

"The original laboratory I joined was very old and it did have some very archaic equipment, shall we say, in terms of the balances were very old, such as the pan and weight balances. When the laboratory was re-located to another part of the factory [it started off under the ballroom], a lot of money was spent on new, more modern equipment... and the work was done in a more accurate way as well."
Martin Calver, Research and Development, on starting in the 1970s.

PROCESSES - 33

Many ex-employees remember a pre-digital world of paper and cash and face-to-face conversation.

"You had to clock in. The clock-in machine was one of those old-fashioned ones. Then someone would sign the cards to say, yes, you're in and nobody's clocked in for you. There was a little hatch, and you had to go and collect your money. I think it was every Thursday. And it came in a little brown envelope. So, at the corner, you would flick through the notes, and think 'yes, that's the coinage' and you got your wages."
Dee Mayling, Factory Worker, 1980s.

"When I first started everything was just manual. We had to log everything in ledgers, and we didn't have any computers to log hours and sickness pay and holiday pay and things like that. Everything was done manually. I used to go around the factory once a week with these clock cards that we took all the hours, the sickness and holiday pay they'd got to get them verified by supervisors."
Jacqueline Parsons, Wages Department, 1970s–1990s.

"No, there was no advertising. I just went to the factory main gate, got an interview with the then chief engineer and got the job just like that. I told them of my experiences and that was good enough. The first day, that was very interesting. You saw a foreman then, not the chief engineer, and the foreman said, 'well there's the steel,' a rack of steel and all sorts of stuff. He says, 'you better make yourself a bench, make yourself a cupboard', and you had to get on with it and do it. I think if you couldn't have done it, they'd have put you straight out the gate."
Ted Luck, Mechanical Engineer, 1980s–1990s.

"I joined as a 16-year-old from school. I'd started to do A Levels and left after a term on point of a stupid principle, probably you'd say in hindsight, and was faced with the task of finding something to do having not given it any thought previously. After Christmas had passed, I went for a couple of interviews in January and I was offered a role as purchasing assistant with Wander Foods. It was all interesting and I felt incredibly young being 16 where a lot of people were considerably older than that. Even the younger ones seemed to be five to ten years older than me, and I seemed to spend all my time wanting to be older than I currently was, to be taken properly seriously. Having said that, I did, as was the fashion of the time, have incredibly long hair. One of the managers used to call me Charles II, which gives you some idea of what I looked like."
Nick Brodrick, Purchasing, 1970s–2000s.

Some recruits joined the factory at a very young age, fresh from school or college.

"Well, it was eight o'clock in the morning, the postman used to bring in the big sacks. We used to have to tip it out, sort the post and put it in the pigeonholes. I went into the offices which was a big building, it is still there now, but if anyone was sick, you honestly had to do the whole lot, go round, do all the engineers, the engineer was here, the factory was up there, and blooming everywhere. It was a long way round I tell you."
Nancy Cox from the Post Room in the 1980s had hundreds of letters to sort, sometimes on a daily basis.

There was scope for young and older workers to progress up the ranks, and the company offered those with promise the opportunity to take courses and training, while still working at the factory.

Martin Calver saw a job for a role in product development in the laboratory in the Evening Echo in 1978 just before his 19th birthday. "I joined in late November and then in the next academic year I started to do day release courses. I did altogether four years of the City and Guilds Food Technician's Certificate. Then I did a Higher Level National Certificate in Food Technology, which was another two years. Altogether I think I probably did about six years' worth of day release courses, which gave me the equivalent qualification of a degree but with the actual practical experience as well."

Ken Allum joined the factory after leaving the marines aged 29 in the 1980s. He began in manufacturing making cardboard boxes. Gradually he came to learn all the processes involved in making Ovaltine, and progressed to become one of the Shift Supervisors, with overall control of the production. "We did do a NEBS course, the National Examination Board of Supervisory Management, that was one of the things we had to do when we got made up to a Shift Supervisor."

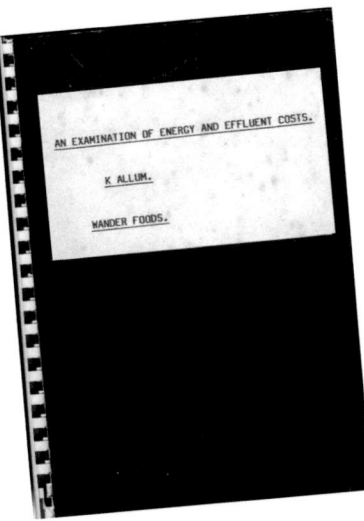

△ This project was completed by Ken Allum as part of his promotion to Shift Supervisor.

△ Ovaltine Research and Development Laboratory, 1971. Photo by Syd Burke.

HEALTH AND SAFETY

"Those early years you could walk up through the bakery and pinch a rusk off the line."
Linda Lythaby, Print Room, 1960s.

"You could go anywhere you liked in the factory... I remember on break-time one of the older trainees he used to lead us out on expeditions around the factory. We actually got right up on the roof."
Roger King, Accounts, 1960s

Health and safety is sometimes treated in a jovial manner in office documents. However throughout its history, the company showed a genuine, paternalistic concern for the welfare of the workers, and this concern increased with the tightening of legislation towards the end of the 20th century.

"As a manager, health and safety was paramount. You were taught everybody has the right to leave work in the same condition they arrived to work in. And so, as a manager, you made sure you had a lot of checks. If there was an accident, there was a big investigation, not to blame someone, but to learn how it could happen."
Peter Addison, Quality Management, 1970s–2000s.

> Dare we use the terrible word "sensible" and implore you girls to wear sensible shoes at work. Think of the pleasure you get when the drudgery of the day is over and you change from the horrible sensible safe shoes into your high fashion. Surely this gives twice the kick compared with wearing fashion all day.
>
> Remember that, although your job may not involve such a risk of foot injury that safety shoes are provided, all jobs carry some risk of tripping, slipping, stumbling and this risk is increased tenfold by wearing unsuitable shoes.
>
> We have some quite pleasant styles of safety shoes which are ideal and a very good bargain, which you can buy if you wish - ask your Supervisor about them and when next you glance through "Vogue" look for the initials R.W.P.

△ A wittily worded notice about the wearing of high heels in the factory from the staff newsletter of 1975.

Dress for the job

Imagine a girl walking through an Arctic blizzard in her underwear, or a fireman fighting a fire in a fur coat, or a policeman making an arrest in a nurses uniform.

Daft isn't it?

But just as you would expect them to wear appropriate clothes for the tasks they are performing, so we expect you to dress sensibly in your job.

Here are a few important tips.

1. All loose ends, such as ties, scarves, belts, must be safely tucked in so that they cannot be caught up in moving machine.
2. Close fitting overalls are best.
3. Wear strong, sensible footwear, preferably with steel toe caps. High heels are lethal, as are opened toed sandals or other
4. If you are issued with goggles or safety helmets, WEAR THEM.
5. Make sure that long hair is well protected under a hat.

6. Leave your jewellery, other than wedding rings, at home.

Specific safety practice

We have listed below some generally accepted good safety practices. Make every effort to learn and practice them in your work.

Do not hesitate TO CAUTION A FELLOW WORKER when he is in danger of being injured because of an unsafe practice.

△ This Health and Safety booklet urges workers to live up to Ovaltine's name as 'the home of good health'.

THE WORLD'S MOST POPULAR FOOD BEVERAGE

From Kings Langley, Ovaltine and its associated products were exported around the globe. 'At Kings Langley we are the biggest single Malt Extract Producer in the world,' writes Chief Executive J.D.G Buchanan in a 1980 company booklet that lists the breadth of its exports to Europe, Africa, Asia, North & South America, and Australia.

This design for a window display for the British Food Fair in 1956 emphasises Ovaltine's place as 'the world's most popular food beverage,' labelling the British Overseas Factories and Kings Langley's global export market.

1980s

PRODUCTS

All of the effort and industry that went on behind the walls of the Kings Langley factory was aimed primarily at making Ovaltine – a warm, malt-based, vitamin-enriched drink that was enormously popular with the public for much of the twentieth century. The Ovaltine product retained a striking appearance in its tin containers made on site in vibrant red or orange and often emblazoned with the figure of the Ovaltine Maid.

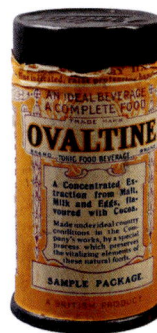

1920s–1930s

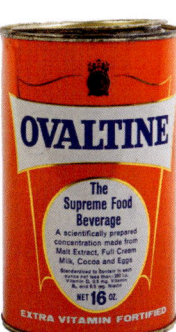

1960s

1970s

"In 1976–7 we were selling bulk ten tonne container loads of Ovaltine to Nigeria on an increasingly regular basis where it was then packed into large 5–7 lb tins at our packing factory in Ikeja. In 1978 I was given the added responsibility of Sales & Marketing Manager for Nigeria and for the next two years spent three weeks per quarter travelling across Nigeria developing the business."

Dr Stephen Fitzpatrick, Research and Development, 1970s–1980s, on the factory's links to Nigeria.

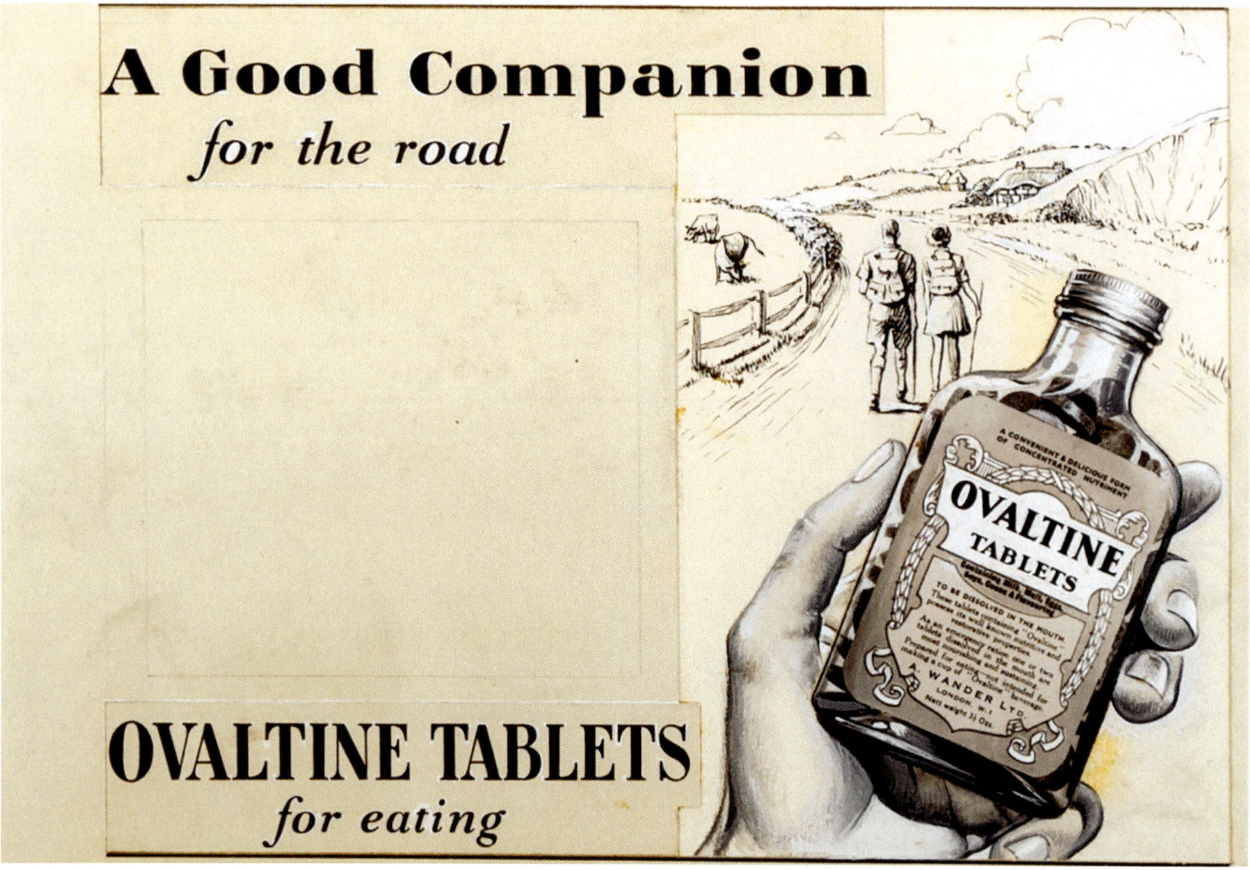

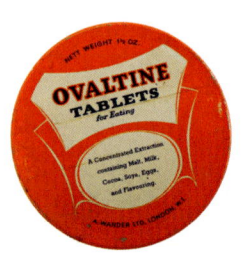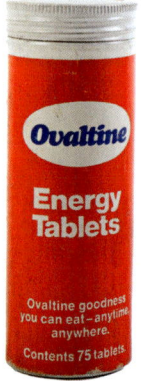

As an accompaniment to the drink, the factory manufactured other products with an Ovaltine base. These 'side' products were said to contain the popular beverage's nutritious properties.

Ovaltine Tablets have an interesting history. They were one of the items included in the ration packs for civilians and soldiers in the Second World War, targeted especially at the Air Force to aid concentration and recovery after long missions. 'As an emergency ration, one or two tablets dissolved in the mouth are most nourishing,' went the wording on the tin.

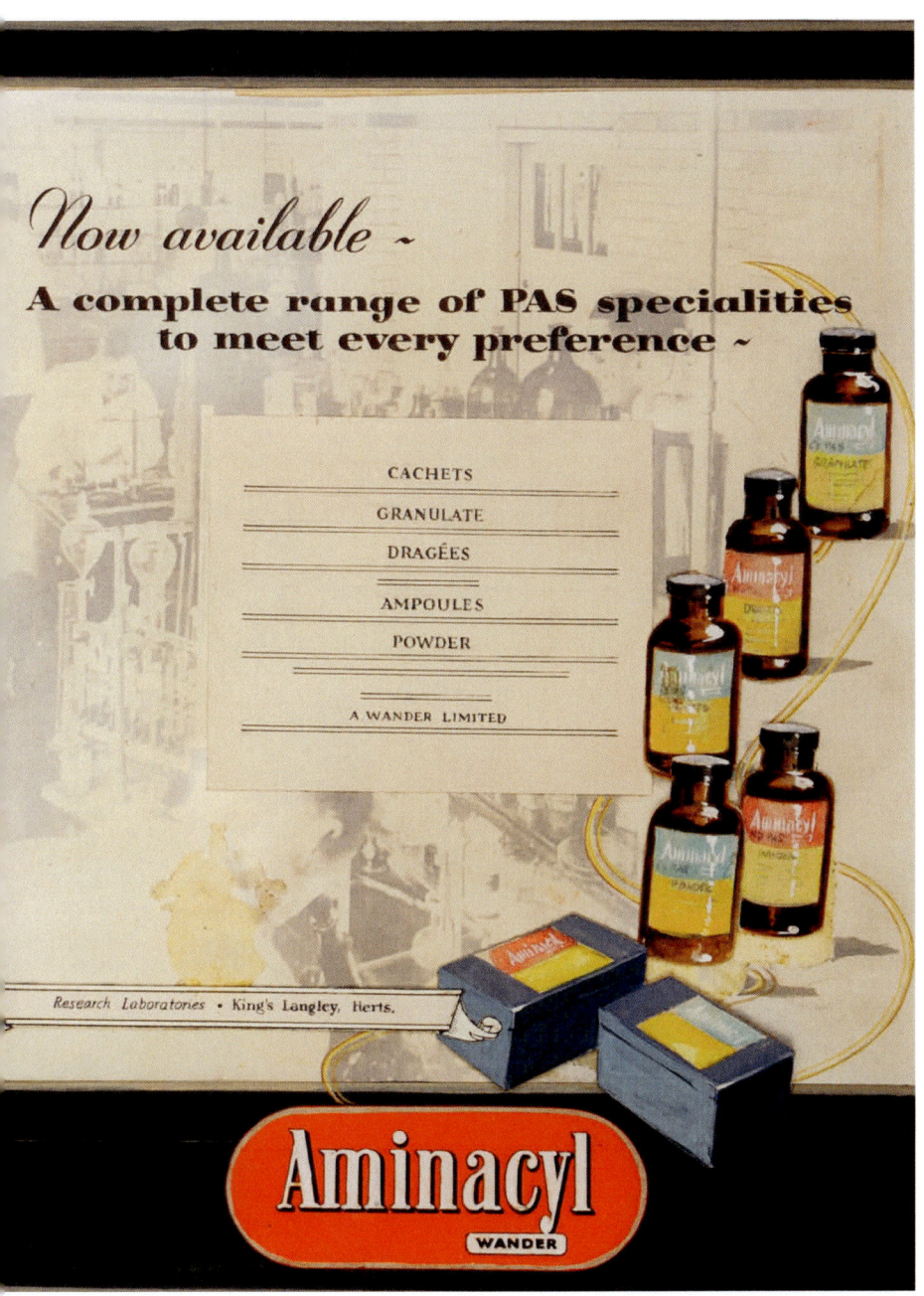

The factory never lost touch with Ovaltine's research and medicinal origins. A range of pharmaceuticals were made on site. In publicity documents these were described as 'products of the famous Ovaltine research laboratories in Kings Langley'. This poster is for Aminacyl which was developed for the treatment of tuberculosis.

Devising lighter alternatives that could be enjoyed by those with dietary needs was one strand of product development, as shown by these chocolate bars 'prepared for diabetics.' The company received awards for its reduced calorie and fat selection.

"We also developed a range of slimming meals called Contour. These were a range of main meals based on dry mixes (like Vesta meals) which gave 450 Kcal per meal as well as one third of your minimum daily requirements of protein, vitamins and minerals. This was 'balanced nutrition' but was ahead of its time as the public just wanted empty calories." *Dr Stephen Fitzpatrick, Research and Development Laboratories, 1970s–1980s.*

The factory was inventive at taking the Ovaltine ingredients and turning them into other baked and powdered products such as biscuits and teething rusks, drinking chocolate, thick shakes and dessert whips. A cold version of Ovaltine was another offering. The factory created a range of chocolates, flavoured and given an extra Ovaltine crunch.

PRODUCTS - 43

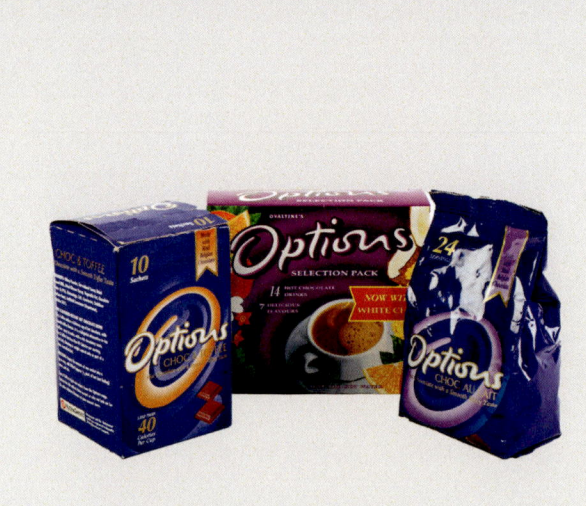

△ Options and Geordie Beer Home Brew Kits were developed on site in Kings Langley by Senior Food Technologist Martin Calver.

"The thing I most enjoyed was the fact that I was in at the starting point for new products that I developed and quite a few of them are still around, for example the Options low calorie flavoured chocolate drinks. That was one of my babies, if you like. A little bit after that I developed an instant version of Ovaltine that was lower calories than the made-with-milk one. I also got involved in the takeover of the homebrew beer kit called Geordie. Wander bought the company. They were based in North Shields, and it was my job to transfer the formulations and the recipes so they could be manufactured in Kings Langley. And from that, it led to me running a telephone advice line, so my name was on all the beer kit instructions, so people could phone up Martin Calver if they had an issue with their beer which left me open to a few pranks from some of my colleagues. On one occasion I was left a message for a phone number that turned out to be Bristol prison. I then fell for another one: 'Can you phone Mr Lyons at this number?' Of course, the number was Whipsnade Zoo."

Martin Calver, Research and Development, 1970s–2000s.

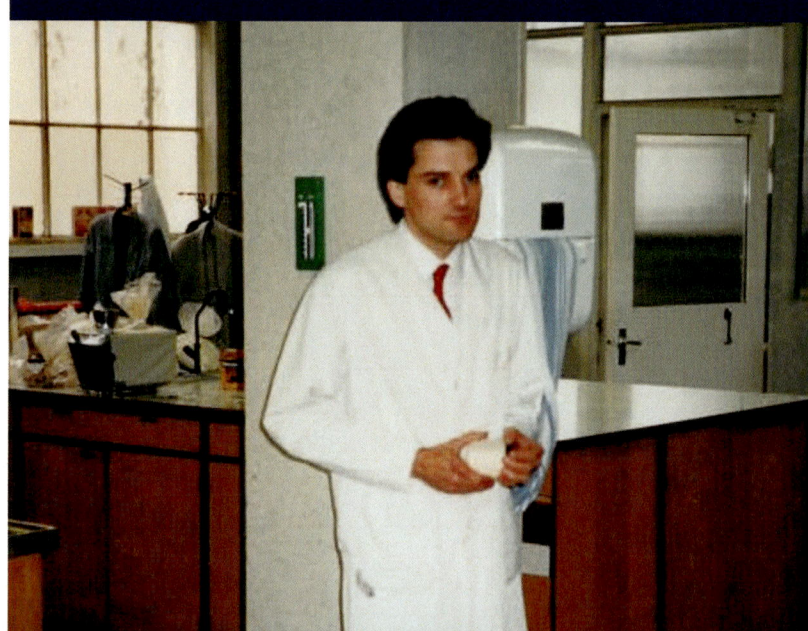

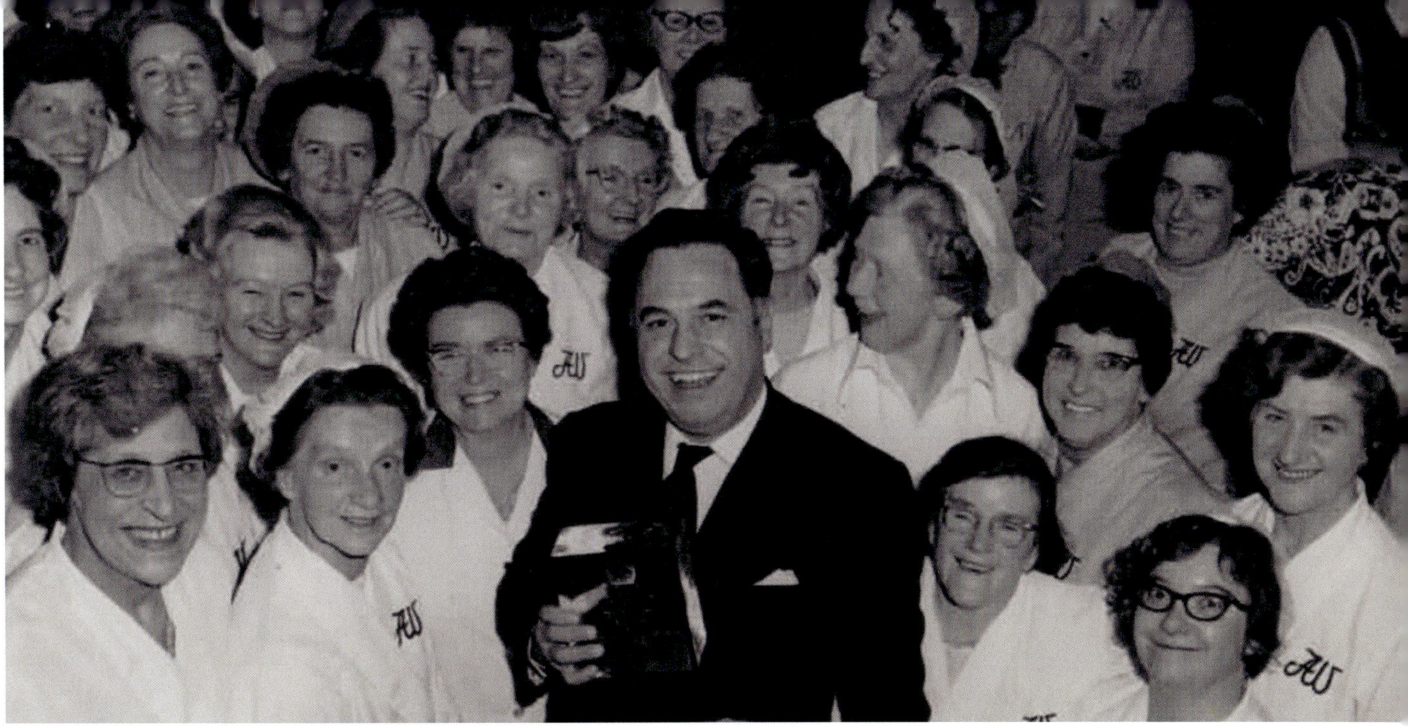

Board of Green Cloth

These are to Certify that by command of

The King

I have appointed

A. Wander Limited

into the place and quality of

Purveyors of Ovaltine

to His Majesty

To hold the said place until this Royal Warrant shall be withdrawn or otherwise revoked

This Warrant is granted to

Sir Harry Hague, Kt.

Lord Chamberlain

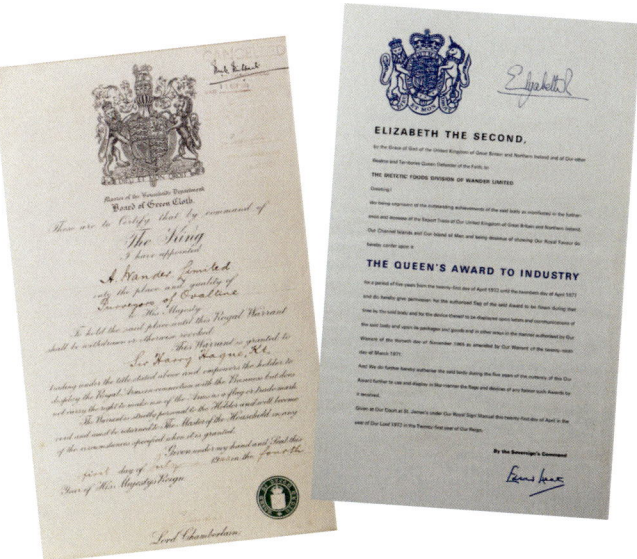

△ Royal Warrant from George VI dated 1 July 1940.

ELIZABETH THE SECOND,

THE DIETETIC FOODS DIVISION OF WANDER LIMITED

Greeting!

THE QUEEN'S AWARD TO INDUSTRY

By the Sovereign's Command

△ The Queen's Award to Industry from Elizabeth II dated 21 April 1972.

ROYAL SEALS OF APPROVAL

Two certificates in the Ovaltine archive were awarded to the company by reigning British monarchs.

This royal warrant to supply Ovaltine to the King is dated 1 July 1940 and may once have hung in a frame on the factory walls. The certificate states that by command of the King, 'I have appointed A. Wander Limited into the place and quality of Purveyors of Ovaltine to his Majesty'.

In 1972, 'the dietetic foods division of Wander Limited' received the Queen's Award to Industry for its achievement in the 'furtherance and increase of the export trade of our United Kingdom of Great Britain and Northern Ireland'.

This was a major award for the company. It was marked by a formal presentation and celebration at the factory, captured in this photograph with Company Chairman Dr Albert Wander surrounded by workers.

ADVERTISING

The advertising archive that was stored at the Kings Langley factory represents almost a century of artistic creativity and determination to keep shoppers stocking their kitchens with Ovaltine and its associated products. Press cuttings, pasted into guard books, begin from the 1910s. Mocked-up and completed artworks sit alongside LPs of radio broadcasts and VHS tapes and film reels of TV advertising. As one office document states, 'Ovaltine's advertisers have never been afraid to have a go at something new'.

△ This press cutting preserved in a company guard book shows an Ovaltine advert that appeared in Punch or The London Charivari in October 1921.

An office document reveals that the company 'remained loyal to their original advertising agency – Saward Baker...and much of the credit for Ovaltine's success must rest with Horace Bury, one of their staff artists'.

'From 1920, Horace Bury...created all Ovaltine advertisements. His distinctive style made Ovaltine ads easily recognisable. For the next forty years he produced well over 2,000 public press and magazine adverts. The company's policy instigated by Harry Hague [Managing Director 1920–1958] was never to repeat an advertisement in any one journal. The enormity of this task can be gauged when you think that Ovaltine advertisements appeared in all women's magazines, all daily and evening papers and about 500 local papers, and regularly in the medical press.'
Novartis – The Ovaltine Story, VHS video.

 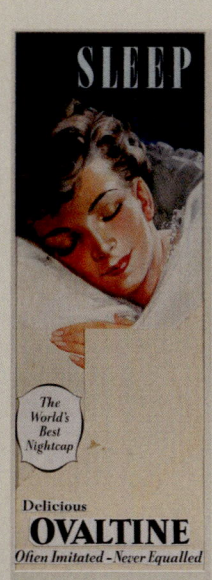 

Ovaltine pitched itself as a drink for the whole family to enjoy. 'Health, strength and energy/ Ovaltine energy... get up and go with Ovaltine' runs the cheerful jingle in a black and white TV advert, with children playing outdoors, fuelled by the malt-based drink.

Children drinking Ovaltine, or eating Ovaltine's biscuits and baby rusks, are recurring marketing motifs, from the company's very beginnings.

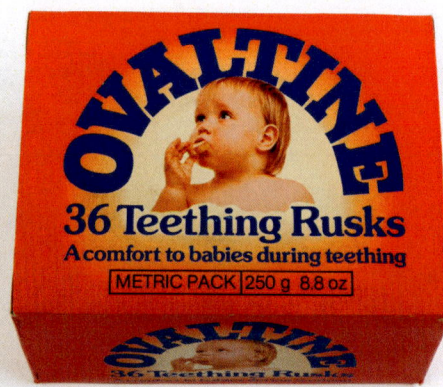

THE OVALTINE MAID

The Ovaltine Maid – instantly recognisable in her red and white dress, with a basket of eggs and sheaf of barley – was a brand character first conceived by the company in the early twentieth century. She smiles radiantly from adverts and products made in Kings Langley. To this day, she decorates the very roof of the factory building, looking out across the railway line.

Female factory workers were often invited to dress as Ovaltine Maids or 'Miss Ovaltine' for the Kings Langley fête and other promotional events. They would wear a costume such as this dress, complete with bustle, apron and bonnet.

△ Joan Bird née Simmonds was selected from the production line to be Miss Ovaltine, circa 1930s.

▷ Two icons: Ovaltine Maids pose with Muhammad Ali on his visit to the factory in 1971.

ADVERTISING · 51

Women were often the 'face' of Ovaltine. We see a variety of 'Ovaltine Girls' throughout the archive, dressed to suit the fashions of the time and to promote both hot and cold versions of the drink.

▷ An Ovaltine girl for the Indian market – showing how the visual motif was adapted to reach consumers around the world.

SPORTS AND SPONSORSHIP

Ovaltine may have been a homely drink, but the company also cultivated another image for the brand – Ovaltine as the fuel for champions and adventurers. Ovaltine sponsored regional and international sporting competitions and was publicly recommended by legends of the twentieth century – from mountaineers to the king of the boxing ring.

▷ Ovaltine sports sponsorship ranged from small, regional events to international competitions. Ovaltine has been the official beverage at many Olympic Games since 1932. During the 1948 Summer Olympics in London, it is said that 25,000 cups were served to competitors at Wembley Stadium.

In 1971, boxing superstar Muhammad Ali promoted the brand on his Ovaltine Autumn Tour, which included appearances at press conferences and supermarkets in towns and cities across the UK, as well as a visit to the factory in Kings Langley. Photographs, press cuttings and programmes reveal a painstakingly planned itinerary by private train carriage. As part of the tour, Ovaltine also flew the sporting hero to Nigeria – a major consumer of the drink produced in Kings Langley.

△ Ovaltine used Radio Luxembourg to broadcast its Ovaltiney Radio Show every Sunday evening at 5.30pm. At the time, the BBC controlled the airwaves and companies had to look to foreign stations to transmit commercial content.

THE OVALTINEYS

Ovaltine was quick to use pioneering forms of technology to promote its products. This is shown in the Ovaltineys Radio Show, first broadcast in December 1934 through Radio Luxembourg. Radios were the household gadget of that era, and the company seized upon the overseas station that would allow them to create their own sponsored programmes. The Ovaltineys was a weekly children's programme, packed with stories, jokes, loveable characters and songs – as well as direct advertising messages: 'Ask Mother for Ovaltine'.

By digitising LP recordings from the collection, we have been able to listen for the first time in decades to the voices of those radio broadcasts, such as the Chief Ovaltiney addressing the millions of children that would come to join the club known as the League of Ovaltineys:

"Greetings to all my Ovaltineys, old and new. You know, children, to me, Sunday is the happiest day of the week, for it is then that I enjoy the very great privilege – the privilege and the happiness – of talking to all my young friends at one and the same time. And, if my words help to bring more boys and girls into our happy league of Ovaltineys then I feel my time has indeed been very well spent. You see, the League of Ovaltineys has a purpose, and that purpose is to bring health, happiness and laughter to all children. Once you are an Ovaltiney you need never be without friends, for your league badge tells your fellow members at a glance that you are an Ovaltiney and therefore a happy, cheery companion..."
Broadcast from December 1938.

△ View of the factory from 1964. Photo by Roger King.

CLOSURE

After almost a century of continuous production, the Ovaltine Factory in Kings Langley was closed in 2002. At its height in the 1950s the workforce was almost 1,500 and generations within the same family worked in its production lines and offices. The closure announcement was received with shock – and genuine grief – among the employees and wider community. The factory occupies a prominent place in Kings Langley, a landmark to locals. While it would not become a listed building, its façade has been preserved. Where once there was machinery and colleagues in the corridors, there are now flats in Ovaltine Court.

"When I was there on my own, it got mighty eerie, because any building makes noises that you're not expecting, and I used to go for a walk just to absorb what I was leaving after all those years."
Peter Addison, Quality Management, on his last months at Ovaltine when most of the workforce had left for good.

"Then obviously trying to find another job when I'd never done a CV in my life. But, the company were really good. We were all sent for retraining, but it was very, very sad. And then once the place closed down and, of course, it's been built on now with houses and flats. I just couldn't go past it for a long, long time. It was almost like I was sort of grieving for the place. I know it sounds a bit strange but that's what it seemed like to me. I just loved it so much. I just didn't want to go."
Jacqueline Parsons, Wages Department, 1970s-1990s.

"We often drove past, when he was alive. We would sometimes go in and park in one of the parking bays, and would look at the factory and go 'right that was the tin shop over there, that was the weigh bridge, they were the offices there', and we would want to get out and, like, walk around the houses."
Dee Mayling on driving by Ovaltine Court with her dad Frank Mayling, who worked at the factory for 20 years as storeman.

▷ One of the thousands of objects rescued from the Ovaltine Factory by the remarkable efforts of the Kings Langley Local History and Museum Society.

RESCUE OF THE OVALTINE ARCHIVE

BY THE KINGS LANGLEY LOCAL HISTORY AND MUSEUM SOCIETY

The remains of the factory are preserved in the Museum Store at Dacorum Heritage thanks to the actions of the Kings Langley Local History and Museum Society. Hearing that the archive was destined for rubbish skips, members of the society began a rescue mission to salvage objects from office walls, boardrooms and the factory archive. Over 10,000 objects were saved, each a precious reminder of the people and history of Ovaltine in the local area.

Five members of the society had one month to complete the task:

"When the history society went into the factory, the building had workmen clearing office items, but, luckily enough, a few paintings had been saved...There were so many items to be archived. Every item taken was written down so eventually it could be properly recorded. There were many offices which contained files, objects, postcards, photographs, which were carefully noted and then boxed to be taken away by the society to be archived. It was a privilege to be involved with the rescue of the Ovaltine as I had known this building all of my life."
Eleanor Broughton, Secretary and Archivist involved in the rescue mission led by the Kings Langley Local History and Museum Society. Eleanor's mother worked in the Tin Shop and her father worked as a Forklift Truck Driver at the factory.

ACKNOWLEDGEMENTS

Dacorum Heritage could not have created this publication without the following, and our sincere thanks go to them all:

The ex-employees of Ovaltine for sharing their memories in written and spoken interviews and helping us to build a picture of the human stories of the factory: Peter Addison, Nick Brodrick, Martin Calver, Sue Chandler, David Evans, Dr Stephen Fitzpatrick, Roger King, Ted Luck, Linda Lythaby, Dee Mayling, Janette Noonan, Jacqueline Parsons, Roy Platten, Beverley Platten and Jan Porter. Particular thanks go to Peter Addison for introducing us to so many former workers.

Sarah Stephens Photography for capturing the Ovaltine collection so beautifully for this book.

The Oral History Volunteers who have helped us to record and preserve these memories: Georgina Johnson, John Lee, Fiona Masters, Jacqueline Palmer, Connie Search and Mike Smith.

The Kings Langley Local History and Museum Society for their advice and support and crucial role in rescuing the Ovaltine archive.

Our Sponsors: the Garfield Weston Foundation and Arts Council England.

A Taste of Ovaltine by Alice Spain and David Spain (2002), invaluable reading for an in-depth history of the Ovaltine Factory in Kings Langley.

FURTHER READING

Dacorum Heritage Online Ovaltine Exhibitions:
dacorumheritage.org.uk

Dacorum Heritage YouTube Channel for a short film on the history of Ovaltine and Ovaltine adverts from the 1950s–1970s:
YouTube @DacHeritage

Dacorum Heritage

Preserving history.
Sharing histories.
Inspiring communities.

Explore the Ovaltine Collection, cared for by Dacorum Heritage. The museum houses over 10,000 objects from the Kings Langley factory that was open from 1913–2002. This 'printed exhibition' offers a glimpse into the collection. Sharing artwork of the iconic factory building and surrounding landscapes, the products made on-site in Kings Langley, and the memories of those who worked in the offices and production lines.

Cover Art:
Watercolour of the Ovaltine Factory in Kings Langley by Gordon Nicholson

PRICE £14

ISBN: 978-0-9540403-0-7

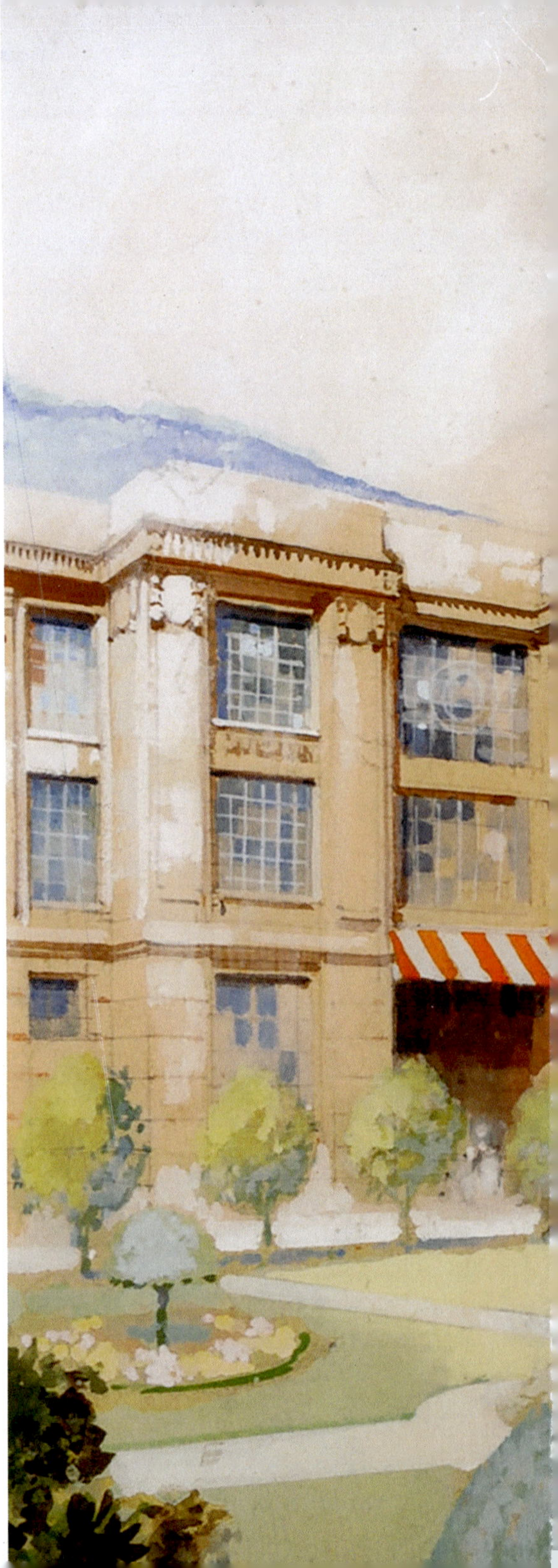